leap of faith

jodi hills

Jodi Hills Publications
www.jodihills.com
New York   Aix en Provence

To Alexandria, Minnesota. Home.

Jodi Hills Publications

I was eight years old when I took my first leap of faith. . . bouncing head first off the diving tower into the wave-rocked waters of Lake Latoka.

I lived in the land of 10,000 lakes.
To be honest, I really only knew three by name —
Lake Le Homme Dieu, Lake Agnes and Lake Latoka.

Lake LeHomme Dieu was nice and clean, with a soft sandy bottom. It was right near my friend Barbie's house. We went there for her birthday. We ate ice cream sandwiches that melted really quickly in the sun and all over our arms, but we just washed off in the lake, and I'm pretty sure we didn't wait an hour after eating.

But Lake LeHomme Dieu, with its inviting, sandy bottom, wasn't very close to my house. Lake Agnes was — Lake Agnes — it didn't even sound like a cool lake. . . and it wasn't. It was dirty and green — I think it was even thick. One of the neighbor boys, who was mean and wild, and got kicked off of our school bus for an entire school year, one time he stuck his foot in Lake Agnes on a dare and pulled it out with seventeen leaches on it. So even though Lake Agnes was right across the gravel road that I lived on, I never went in it. Which brings me to my favorite of the 10,000, or three, Lake Latoka.

I could ride my flowered banana seat bike to Lake Latoka in about 20 minutes. If the wind wasn't against me, I could ride in about 19. Once, I think I did it faster... but I can't be sure, because it was on the day that my watch — that I ordered from the Bazooka bubble gum wrappers — stopped working. That watch only lasted three days... but they were three good days, especially the day it came in the mailbox.

Anyway, it felt really fast this one day when I was riding... almost as if I was going to fly. I picked up speed on the hill right before the left turn to the lake. The wind was at my back, pushing me and pushing me. My hair was dancing behind my neck, the handlebar streamers were like rockets, and my banana seat cut through the air like a knife. My hands held their grips like never before and I knew that if I stuck my feet out at just the right moment, the wind would pick me up and this would be the day that I would fly... this would be the day that my feet would touch the sky.   But it wasn't.

It was actually the day, I lost one of my bumper tennis shoes. I knew I should have double knotted them before I tried to fly. It still may have been the fastest I ever rode to Lake Latoka. And I knew on that day, that it must feel very good to fly.

I carried my beach towel to the lake in my bike's basket. The white wicker had flowers on it, just like the banana seat.

I loved that bike.

It was the greatest. All my friends loved it. But I didn't even need a lock for it. Nobody ever stole bikes from the beach. It was kind of like our sacred ground... and we knew that in order to get to our sacred ground, you had to have a bike, and to take that away from someone, to take away their chance to fly on the way to that glorious one of 10,000 lakes, well that would just be a terrible crime, so we didn't do it.

I don't think I realized how beautiful life without mistrust really was...

How could I know?

You can't...

until it is taken away —

and only in those rare moments,

when you let yourself

remember innocence,

can you feel the slip of beauty.

Lake Latoka had two diving towers. They were out maybe three miles from shore... OK, maybe just 50 yards or so, but it was really deep out there... maybe three miles deep... well, it was way over my head anyway. One tower had an actual diving board, the other was just a platform. The two towers were perched 10 feet above the water. Each tower was held up by four slimy poles — not Lake Agnes kind of slime, but more of a friendly, somewhat slippery kind. Both had a ladder, with twelve rights of passage steps, topped with a glorious, green carpeted platform.

I had watched the kids out on the towers for several years. They seemed so smart, and brave and old... after all, they were teenagers. The teen-tanned girls flirted with the boys in their denim cut-offs and they flirted back by pushing each other off. They did that on both towers, but they did something on the diving tower that intrigued me the most. They did bouncers — that's what I called it anyway.

It was like they were flying... one, two, three running steps, then a giant bounce at the end of the diving board... bending the board way down, then flinging them up through the clouds, and with arms in front of them they would cut through the water head first. It was beautiful. It was glorious. It lured me and scared me to death. I stood in safety of shallow waters and knew that I would do a bouncer, but I didn't know how or when.

It was a cloudy day, near the end of June. I had been to the beach twice since I had made my vow to bounce, but I hadn't yet made it past the buoys that marked the deeper water. Once, I went with my neighbor Kathy, but she didn't seem really interested. And once I went with my neighbor David. David was kind of frail and pale, and stuck mostly to the shade. I'm not sure why he came. He never did again. But this was the cloudy day, near the end of June. The clouds had kept the crowd to a minimum. The towers were nearly empty.

This was my chance, and I was going to take it.
Armed with nothing but my baby fat and a
child-like courage, I walked out to the buoys.
I took three deep breaths and dove under them,
came up for air, almost surprised that I had
started my journey, and then began to swim...

Crawl stroke,

crawl stroke,

side to side,

watch where you're going,

don't forget to breathe,

I'm doing it, I'm doing it,

I'm really going to make it...

One of the big boys swam right past me, but I didn't care... I was still going to make it.

Look at me, look at me Mister Lifeguard, I'm going out to the tower, don't worry, crawl stroke, crawl stroke, I'm going to make it.

There it was, right in front of me, the ladder, I was going to make it. I reached out on my final stroke and grabbed the beautiful metal. I had made it. I clung to the bottom rung, all smiles, prideful, and out of breath.

"Well, are you goin' up already?" asked the impatient teen behind me. I didn't know . . . I hadn't thought that far ahead. . . I was so happy to have made it this far. . . Was I going up? It was such a big tower. . . it looked bigger from below. . . a lot smaller from shore.

Could I actually make it up the steps?

She pushed me aside and started climbing the ladder.

I'm OK. . . I'm OK, treading water, treading water. . . I can do this for three minutes. . . we had lessons in the pool. . . still OK. . . alright, she's gone. Grab the ladder, grab the ladder.

It was now or never. I had to climb the ladder. But I knew if I climbed the ladder, I would have to jump off, maybe not dive off, but at least jump off. There would be no climbing back down the ladder. Nothing was more shameful. I heard of one boy once who did, and I think they made him and his family move out of town. Hand up, foot up, hand up, foot up, I was climbing the ladder.

Look, I'm climbing. I'm really doing it. . . I'm going up.

I put one foot on the wet, green carpet and then the other foot. There I was, frozen at the top of the tower. I had done it. I had climbed the ladder. I could see for a thousand miles. . . or at least to shore. . . it was very far. It was beautiful. I could hear boats and kids screaming and splashing, and trees swaying and waves rustling, and fish blowing bubbles. . . I could hear and see it all. . . everything was so clear from that glorious, wet, green carpeted throne. This was my moment.

I was a foot shorter than the three other kids on the tower, but I was queen of the world.
My one piece navy sailor swimsuit was my gown and I could rule all. . . I was. . .AAAAAAAAHHH . . . flung off the side like a peasant. I hit the water with a surprising slap. . . and sank.

It's over my head,

it's over my head. . .

kick and climb, kick and climb. . .

it's just like the deep end of the pool. . .

oooooh, ick!

weeeeds. . .

kick and climb. . . up. . . up. . .

kick and climb. . .

my head thrust above the water. . .

I'm ok... I'm doing it...

it's over my head, but I'm doing it...

tread that water,

where's the tower,

spin around...

there it is,

grab a pole... hang on,

kind of slimy, kind of nice...

I'm OK... I made it...

hanging on to the pole.

Sometimes decisions get made for you. The good news was I didn't have to climb down the ladder. It wasn't glamorous. It was no bouncer, but I had made it up and off the tower and I knew I would go again.

I went back every day. I was a pretty good swimmer, and getting better. I could go on either tower. I could jump off. Sometimes I was still pushed, but I didn't really care... I was part of it ... the action, the thrill, the sun, the wind, the wet flung hair... yeah... it was summer, and I was kid on a tower... yeah, I was a kid who jumped off a tower... I hadn't made it to the diving board yet, but I wasn't worried...

summer

was

never

going

to

end.

I was wet and wind blown through mid August.
I rode one tassel right off of my handle bars.
I got a plastic camera from Bazooka Joe. When
I was riding to Olson's Super Market to get film, I
dropped it on the road and ran over it myself with
my back tire. I still think it might have been a good
camera.

I rode my bike home, singing the super market
theme song,

"Olson's Super market,
bring your car and park it, S & H green stamps,
Olson's super market..."

"Bring your car and park it" — now those were
some beautiful lyrics — and I thought I was
simple ... and S & H green stamps — please...
my Bazooka Joe gum wrappers were much better,
and speaking of which, I checked the mail box
every day, just in case I'd get my next arrival.

I loved getting mail in the summertime. . . I was a kid on my bike in the sun, gettin' mail . . . but this time it was different — No one was more surprised than I was to get the letter saying that school would be starting in two weeks.

School... I hadn't seen that coming.

Two weeks left.
I was yet to do a bouncer.

Sure I had swum further than most 8 year olds,
been pushed off, even jumped from the tower, but
I had never taken the dive... and there wasn't much
time left.

Two more weeks and I'd again be behind the desk
and behind Mrs. Erickson. Mrs Erickson... again.

She was my second grade teacher and then decided
to switch grades and now I was going to have her
again in third.

Another year of Mrs. Erickson, with her stick
pointing and heavy make-up. I just knew I couldn't
sit through another year of all that sameness
without having tried something new. I had to do
a bouncer. I just had to.

"Mrs. Erickson again... Mrs. Erickson again..."
— it became my mantra as I swam out to the tower. With a new found strength bred out of aggravation, I stepped onto the diving board. It was soooo unstable. It was like a stick of Jello ...a board made of Knox Blox... it jiggled like a Christmas belly and their was nothing to hang on to. My feet begged my knees for stability. How did they do it? I could barely walk. How could they jump? I couldn't think. I could barely see. I couldn't hear... and thank goodness for that, because the line of teenage boys behind me had learned a lot of new words that summer that were far from encouraging. They began to jump up and down. It was their way of keeping the line moving. The board shook, my knees buckled and without fanfare I fell into the water... not the splash I was hoping to make. I hung on to the pole just beneath the diving board. I watched them fly over me for hours. They looked so light and free. I felt heavy, like a rock. The only thing longer than my swim back to shore was my bicycle ride back home.

I played with David for the next three days. He had a big mound of dirt beside his house and liked to play with trucks and diggers. I tried to convince myself that I liked being with David... that it was fun playing on his big, safe dirt pile... that it was cool that he could touch his nose with his own tongue... that I didn't really even want to go back to the lake... that I wasn't really scared. But after three days of staying in the shade of David's mound I realized that I was just kidding myself, I was avoiding the lake because I was afraid ... and not only that I was really, really dirty, and needed a swim.

Pale David got smaller in my rear-view mirror as I biked away. It wasn't the fastest I ever rode... but I was riding again, and going to the lake. I swam past the buoys and climbed the ladder. I stood at the end of the line and watched each one dive off in front of me. I knew diving was hard... but we had been taught at the Central School Pool. The teacher held our legs at the edge of the pool, so our heads would go in first.

I could dive. I could do this.

I got closer in line.

They were flying off in front of me. What was I going to do? Sit on a dirt pile for the rest of my life?

I got closer to the board.

Only three in front of me now.

Sure it was going to be hard. But it was flying — was that supposed to be easy?
I could do this. I could really do it.

One left now and I would be next. I was really going to do it. I had a banana seat bike for goodness sake. I was going to be a third grader. I rode on a major road just to get here.

I can do this. I can do a bouncer.

The girl in front of me was gone. There was no more time to think. . . my heart pounded fast and steady as if leading me to the edge of the board. . . I lifted my right leg and ran.

One, two, three and I jumped!

It was almost in slow motion as the board bent beneath me and then flung me straight in the air. . .

It was me. I was flying.

There were no longer obstacles or worries, just a beautiful blue sky all around me.

I was flying and I was free. And it's funny, at that moment, I didn't feel smarter or older, or more brave, like I thought the others did, or I would, but what I felt was really happy. . .

happy to be me.

I had thought on that one day in June, when I rode my bike the fastest, that it must feel really good to fly... and it does.

My hands shot above my head and I cut through the water.

I had done my first bouncer!

I knew I could face anything — even the sameness of third grade at Washington Elementary.

That was my first leap of faith. I thought I've had so many since, but maybe I've just had chances . . . maybe I've just had the towers . . . towers of friendships and schooling, death and divorce, diseases battled and games won, loves gained and lost, tears and smiles and laughter and jobs and waiting.

Maybe they get harder to see now, or maybe I just turn away, but I don't want to just swim out to the towers. I don't want to live like that. I want to jump toward my leaps. I want to believe in my faith. I want to get in over my head, and kick and thrash — and, if I need to — cling to the most unlikely stable, slimy forces. When I dream, I want to climb every slippery step. I want to hope and believe three miles deep. I want to trust my unlocked feelings. And when I love and when I live, I want to take three running steps and get airborne.

I don't know if this is going to be the

day that my feet will touch the sky . . .

but I am going to climb that tower,

and I'm going to be scared

and I'm going to be happy

and with the wind in my hair,

my heart is going to lead me . . .

and one way or another,

I am going to fly!